Preface

Efforts made in recent years to provide a wider choice of reading material for children have been warmly welcomed by teachers. Experience has shown that reading material which allows for horizontal rather than vertical movement is of paramount importance. This series aims to provide such material in the form of stories, carefully selected for their appeal to children and for their significance in the traditions and cultures of the major world religions.

Stories from World Religions, obviously not a course in religious education, can usefully supplement the material in any agreed syllabus. While it emphasises Christianity, as the religion that has shaped our national life, its aim is to introduce children to the major religions as the living beliefs of other peoples of our world.

Religious truth is conveyed as much through stories as through historical events. This series therefore aims to introduce children to the different kinds of story used in religion—myth, history, legend, parable, festival—and to help children to a progressive under-standing of them so that they can apprehend the truths conveyed.

The controlled vocabulary and language structure have been carefully graded to make Book 1 most suitable for reading ages 7–8 years; Book 2 for 8–9 years; Book 3 for 9–10 years; and Book 4 for 10–11 years. This has been achieved by testing each story theoretically with a recognised readability analysis, and in practice by testing with children of the appro-priate reading ages.

Norman J. Bull
Reginald J. Ferris

Where to Find the Stories

WIDE RANGE
Stories from World Religions

1

Norman J. Bull
Reginald J. Ferris

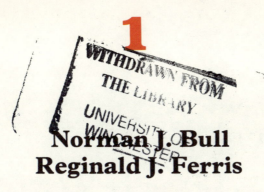

Oliver & Boyd

Illustrated by Annabel Large

OLIVER & BOYD
Robert Stevenson House
1–3 Baxter's Place
Leith Walk
Edinburgh EH1 3BB
A Division of Longman Group Ltd.

First published 1982

ISBN 0 05 003370 0

Set in 14/20 pt. Plantin 110
Printed in Hong Kong by
Sheck Wah Tong Printing Press Ltd.

Brave Muskrat

Men and women have always wondered
about the beginning of our world.
They wanted to know how it began
and where things came from.
   People in different places
made up different stories
about the beginning of the world.
This is one of them.
It was told by the Indian people
who lived in the forests of America
many years ago.

In the beginning
there was nothing but water.
There was no world and no land.
There were no trees.
There were no people.
There was only sea.
But on the sea there was a raft
and on this raft sat Wisakedjak
and his three friends.
They were Beaver, Muskrat
and Loon the diver bird.
There was nowhere for them to go
and nothing for them to do.

At last Wisakedjak got tired
of doing nothing
and then he had an idea.

"I will make a world,"
he said to his friends.
"I will make land and trees,
and I will make people too.
But before I can make this world
I need some mud, and the only mud
is at the bottom of the sea."

Wisakedjak was lazy
and he was a coward too.
He was not going to dive down
to the bottom of the sea
for some mud.
Besides, Wisakedjak's friends
could swim and dive.
They were not afraid of the water.
So Wisakedjak looked at Loon
and he said to his friend,

"Loon, you are a diver.
See if you can dive
to the bottom of the sea
and bring up some mud for me.
Then I can start to make my world."

Loon took a deep breath
and dived straight down into the water.
Down and down he dived.
Deeper and deeper he went.
At last he could see
the bottom of the water.
But his breath was gone
and his lungs felt as if

they were bursting.
Loon had to come up quickly
to get more air.
He only just managed
to get back to the raft.
Loon flopped on the raft,
gasping for breath.
His strength was gone
and he could do no more.

Then Wisakedjak looked at Beaver
and said,
"You are a fine swimmer.
You are a hard worker too.
See if you can dive
to the bottom of the sea
and bring up some mud for me.
Then I can start to make my world."
Beaver flipped into the sea.
He was not a fine diver like Loon,
but he was a fine swimmer.
Down and down he pushed.
Lower and lower he went.
At last he could see
the bottom of the water.
He could see the bottom,
but he could not reach it,
for all his breath was gone.
He could go no deeper
and he knew he must come up for air.
Beaver only just managed
to get back to the raft safely.
He could do no more.

Now only Muskrat was left.
Wisakedjak said to his friend, Muskrat,
    "You too are a fine swimmer.
See if you can dive
to the bottom of the sea
and bring up some mud for me.
Then I can start to make my world."
    "I will try," said Muskrat.
"I am not a fine diver, like Loon.
I am not a hard worker, like Beaver.
But, as you say, I am a good swimmer.
I will do my best."
    Down and down swam Muskrat.
Deeper and deeper he pushed.
At last he could see
the bottom of the water.
He could see the bottom,
but he could not reach it,
for all his breath was gone.
He could go no deeper
and he knew he must come up for air.
Muskrat came back to the raft,
gasping for air.

No one said a word.

There was nothing to say.

There was nothing to do.

Without the mud,

Wisakedjak could not make his world.

So they just sat there.

Loon looked at Beaver.

Muskrat looked at Wisakedjak.

Then brave Muskrat spoke.

"I was so close to the bottom," he said.

"I want to try again."

Into the water he went.

Down, down, down,

deeper and deeper he went.

But again he came back without the mud.

He had not reached the bottom.

All his breath was gone

and he was tired and weak.

Muskrat rested for a time.

Then he got up again

and said bravely,

"I will have one more try."

Muskrat dived into the water again.

He was gone for a long time and
his friends began to worry about him.
They waited and waited,
but still Muskrat did not come back.

Then Wisakedjak saw some bubbles
in the water.
He put his hand down
and found poor brave Muskrat.
He was dead.

Muskrat had died before he could get
back to the raft.
But his paw was tightly closed
and there was something in it.
In Muskrat's paw
there was a tiny ball of mud
from the bottom of the sea.
Brave Muskrat had found the mud
and brought it back to the raft.
Now Wisakedjak could start
to make his world.

First he made islands.
Then he made big lands.
He made mountains and flat lands.
He made trees and plants.
He made animals and insects.
He made men and women for his world.
Wisakedjak made all these things
from the tiny ball of mud
which brave Muskrat brought up
from the bottom of the sea.

The Rainbow Bridge

Long ago, in the cold lands of the North,
there lived people called Norsemen.
They were strong and brave
and their Gods were strong
and brave too.

The God they loved best
was Thor the Thunderer.
Thor was God of Thunder
and Lightning
and Storm.

People called him
Mighty Thor because
he was so big and strong
and powerful.

Mighty Thor protected the other Gods

and all the people of the Northlands.
He protected them from all dangers
with his great hammer, the Thunderbolt.
The children of the Northlands
grew up to be strong and brave.
They wanted to be like Thor the Thunderer.

*   *   *   *   *   *

In the Northlands
there lived a boy named Olaf.
Olaf was the son of Harald Fork-Beard.
Harald was a brave man
and Olaf wanted to be like his father
when he grew up.
    Olaf's father had a boat,
and sometimes he took Olaf with him
when he went out in it.
One day when Olaf and his father
were out in the boat,
there was a great storm.
The storm roared and thundered
and the sky became darker and darker.

"Look, Olaf," said his father.
"Thor is angry."
Olaf looked up at the dark sky.
He was afraid.
But suddenly the sky brightened
and a beautiful rainbow appeared.
It stretched across the sky
between earth and heaven.
Olaf had never seen anything so beautiful.
"Father," he asked, "what is that?"

Harald Fork-Beard looked at the sky
and answered his son's question.

"That is Bifrost, Olaf," he said.

"What is it for?" asked Olaf.

"It is the bridge between earth
and heaven," his father said.
"It is made of earth and fire and water."

Then Olaf asked another question.

"Can anyone go over the bridge
and get to heaven, Father?"

"No," said his father.
"Only the Gods can use the bridge.
They ride across it on their horses.
But there is one God
who cannot use the Rainbow Bridge.
He is Thor the Thunderer.
Mighty Thor is too huge and heavy.
The bridge would fall down
if he thundered across it.
So he has to wade through the deep waters
which flow underneath the bridge."

Olaf thought about all the things
his father had told him.

There was still more he wanted to know
about the bridge.

"Are there any men
who can cross the bridge?" he asked.
His father shook his head and said,

"No living men can cross the bridge.
But there are some who can cross it
after they have died.
They are the heroes, the men
who have died bravely in battle.
These heroes are taken over the bridge
to heaven.   They live there for ever
in the Hall of Heroes."

      ★   ★   ★   ★   ★   ★

The storm was over now
and the sea was still.
The rainbow had gone,
but Olaf went on thinking about
the bridge of beautiful colours.

At last it was time for them
to return home, and Olaf's father

turned the boat towards the shore.
Olaf asked another question.

"Father, how do the Gods make sure
that no one else crosses the bridge?"

"The bridge is guarded," said his father.
"It is guarded by the God of Light,
who lives in the rocks beside the bridge.
He is the Watchman of the Gods
and he keeps watch all day and all night.
If there is danger,
he blows on his Ringing Horn.
The Horn sounds loud and long
and it can be heard all over heaven
and all over earth.

"The God of Light has sharp eyes
and he can see what is happening
in the far, far distance.
He can see by night as well as by day.
His ears are very sharp, too.
He can hear the grass growing
in the ground!
He can hear the wool growing
on the backs of sheep!

The God of Light
is always watching
and always listening.
He knows when danger is near.
His sharp eyes see it
and his sharp ears hear it.
Whenever danger is near
he warns the other Gods
by blowing loud and long
 on his Ringing Horn.''

Olaf had just one more question.

"Do the Gods have enemies
just as our people have enemies?"
he asked.

"Yes," answered his father.
"The Gods have fierce and powerful enemies.
Their enemies are the Giants—
Frost Giants,
Fire Giants
and Rock Giants.
They all live in Giant Land,
across the sea.
These Giants are always waiting
and watching for a chance
to attack the Gods.

"But the God of Light is always watching
too.   He guards the Rainbow Bridge
and he warns the Gods of danger
by blowing on his Ringing Horn.
When Thor hears that warning sound
he knows that danger is near.
Then Mighty Thor comes
to protect us all with his Thunderbolt.

He will always be there
to protect us from the Giants."

★   ★   ★   ★   ★   ★

This story tells us
how the Norsemen believed
that the rainbow was a bridge.
They believed it was a bridge
between earth and heaven.
  Other people believed this too.
People who lived on islands
in the South Seas
said that the rainbow was a ladder.
Men who had become heroes on earth
climbed up the rainbow ladder
to win their prize in heaven.
  In many lands
men believed that all good people
crossed over the Rainbow Bridge
when they died,
to live for ever in heaven.

A Baby in Danger

We all like to hear stories
about our favourite heroes
and the things they did long ago.
This story is about
the birth of Moses,
a great leader of the Jews.
Moses was a real person,
but we cannot be sure
that this story is about
something that really happened to him.
Stories like these grew up long ago
and were passed on from person to person
until someone wrote them down.
Stories like these are called legends.

*   *   *   *   *   *

Once there was a little girl
whose name was Miriam.
She lived with her father and mother
in the land of Egypt.

Miriam's family belonged to the Hebrew
people who had lived happily in Egypt
for many years.
But now there was a new king in Egypt
who did not like the Hebrews.

"There are too many of these Hebrews
living here," he said to the people
of Egypt. "They are strangers
in our land.
One day they might turn against us
and become our enemies.

We must do something quickly
before it is too late."

Then the new king of Egypt
gave a cruel order.
He said,

"Every girl baby of the Hebrews may live,
but every boy baby of the Hebrews must
die.   They must be thrown into the river to
drown."

When Miriam heard about the king's order
she was afraid and very worried.
Her mother had a new baby.
The baby was a boy
and if the Egyptians saw him
they would throw him into the river.

At first Miriam helped her mother
to hide the baby.
When he was little it was not hard
to keep him secret.
But when the baby began to grow bigger
it became harder and harder
to hide him in their home.

Then Miriam's mother

thought of another way to hide him.
She took some leaves from the bulrushes
which grew tall and strong
in the water by the river.
She made a little basket with these leaves.
Then she made a lid to cover it.
She put thick mud from the river
all over the outside of the basket.
When the mud was dry and hard
she covered it with tar.
This was to keep out the water.
When the basket was finished
it was warm and dry inside
and hard and strong on the outside.

Miriam and her mother put the baby boy
in the basket and covered it with the lid.
Then Miriam's mother hid the basket
in the thick bulrushes by the river.
Miriam hid nearby
to watch over the baby in the basket.

As Miriam watched,
an Egyptian princess came past.
She had come down to the river to wash.
When she saw the basket,
hidden in the bulrushes,
she wondered what it could be.
She took the lid off the basket
and there she saw the baby.
The baby began to cry
and the princess felt sorry for him.

She took him into her arms
and wished that he was her own baby.

"Look," said the princess to her maid.
"It's a baby boy.
It must be one of the Hebrew children."

Then Miriam came out from her hiding
place.   She went up to the Egyptian
princess and bowed before her.

"Would you like me
to find a Hebrew woman
to nurse the baby for you?" she asked.

"Yes," said the princess.
"Bring me a nurse from the Hebrews
to look after the baby for me."

Miriam hurried home
and came back with her mother.
"Take this baby to your home,"
said the princess.
"Nurse him for me
and I will pay you well."
So Miriam's mother took him home
and became the nurse of her own baby.
She had no need to hide him now
because she was nursing him for the princess.
No one would throw the baby
of an Egyptian princess into the river.
Miriam was not worried any more
because she knew that her baby brother
was safe from harm.

When the baby grew into a boy
he no longer needed a nurse.
His mother took him to the princess.
How happy the princess was
to have the child for her own.
"I will call him Moses," she said.
"He will be my son."
So Moses became the son

of the Egyptian princess
and lived with her in the royal palace.

*   *   *   *   *   *

This legend about the baby Moses
is a very old one.
It tells how Moses, the Hebrew baby,
was brought up as an Egyptian.
But Moses never forgot
that he belonged to the Hebrew people,
and when he grew up
he became the great leader
of the Hebrew people.

The Shepherd Boy who Became King

Long after the time of Moses,
the leader of the Jews
was a king called David.
This story is about
David the shepherd boy,
before he became
David the King.

*   *   *   *   *   *

In the land we now call Israel
there lived a farmer named Jesse.
He lived in the little town of Bethlehem
with his wife and sons.
Jesse had eight sons
and they all helped their father
on the farm.
One day a stranger came to Bethlehem
to visit Jesse and his sons.

The visitor's name was Samuel
and he was a wise and holy man.
For many years Samuel had been
the great leader of the people of Israel.
He had chosen a king
to lead them in battle
against their enemies.

The king's name was Saul.
He was brave and strong,
and taller than any other man
in the land of Israel.

Saul could fight well
but he was not a good king
and Samuel was sorry he had chosen him.

Now Samuel wanted to find
a new king for his people
and he had come to Bethlehem
to choose him.
One of the sons of Jesse
would be the next king,
but Samuel did not know which one.

So Samuel went to see Jesse
and asked to see his sons.
First, Jesse brought his eldest son
to see Samuel. The eldest son
was tall and strong
but Samuel was sure
that he was not the next king.
Then Jesse brought his second son
to see Samuel.
He too was tall and strong
but when Samuel saw him he said,
"No, this is not the one to be king."
So Jesse brought his third son.

Again Samuel knew he was not the one.
Jesse brought seven sons to Samuel
and each time Samuel said,
   "No, this is not the one."
Then Samuel asked Jesse,
   "Are these all the sons you have?"
   "No," said Jesse.
"There is one other.
You have seen all my sons
except David, the youngest one.
He is on the hills of Bethlehem
looking after my sheep."
When Samuel heard this he said,
   "Send your servant to find him.
We will not sit down to eat
until I have seen your son David."
   At last the servant found David
and brought him to Samuel.
David was a fine, strong lad
with red hair and shining blue eyes.
At once Samuel was sure
that this shepherd boy
was the one to be the next king.

He took from his belt
a goat's horn filled with olive oil.
Samuel poured some of it
over David's head.
He did this to show that David
would be the next king of Israel.
 Then David went back
to the hills of Bethlehem
to look after his sheep, and to wait.
He was content to carry on
looking after his father's sheep.

But he knew that when the right time came
he would become the king
of the people of Israel.

★   ★   ★   ★   ★   ★

David loved to be with his sheep.
He knew them all by name.
They knew his voice and
came when he called.
   Every morning
David called to his sheep
and led them out of the fold.
He led them to where
there was green grass to eat.
When the sun grew hot
he found a place for them to rest
under shady trees.
They needed cool water to drink
but running water frightened them.
So David found a quiet stream
where the water was still and calm.
Here he sat down to eat the food

he had brought with him.

After he had eaten,
David picked up his harp.
He liked to make music and to sing,
and he carried his harp with him
wherever he went.
David's harp was small
and easy to carry.
It was made of hard wood
and it had eight strings.
He could play it with one hand.

For a while he played
and then it was time to practise
with his sling.
His sling was for throwing stones
and David had made it himself
from a piece of leather.
It had a strong string at each end.

David stood up
and untied the sling from his belt
where he always carried it.
Then he picked up some smooth, round
stones.   Now he was ready to practise.

First he chose a tree to throw at.
Then he put a stone in his sling
and held it by the two strings
in his hand.
He spun the sling round his head.
Round and round it went,
faster and faster.
Suddenly he let go of one of the strings.
The stone flew towards the tree.
It hit the tree just where
David meant it to hit.
That was because David practised
with his sling every day.
He had to be sure he never missed.

David used his sling to warn
the sheep and lambs in his flock.
Sometimes a little lamb wandered away
from the other sheep.
Then David threw a stone from his sling
to warn the lamb.
He made the stone land
just in front of the lamb's nose.
This frightened the lamb
and it ran back to its mother
and was safe again.

Sometimes a wild beast
crept after the flock
and waited for a sheep
to wander off by itself.
Sometimes a jackal came after the sheep.

Sometimes it was a lion or a bear.
When David saw any wild beast
near his sheep,
he let fly with his sling.
His stone hit the beast on its head
and it ran away in fright.

Before night time came,
David led his sheep back to the fold.
The fold had strong stone walls
with thorn bushes on top.
No wild beast could get over the walls
into the fold and the sheep were safe
there for the night.

The only way into the fold
was through a small gap in the wall.
As the sheep went through the gap

David counted them, one by one.
He had to make sure
that no sheep were missing.
As well as counting his sheep,
David looked carefully to see
if they had any cuts or scratches.
He rubbed olive oil into their cuts
before he let them into the fold.

When all the sheep were inside the fold,
they were safe for the night.
David wrapped himself in his thick cloak
and lay across the gap in the wall.
David himself was the door.
No wild beast could get past him,
for he was a good shepherd boy.
He guarded his sheep by night
as well as by day.

As David lay there
he thought of an idea for a new song.
He thought to himself,
   "God is like me.
He loves his people
as I love my sheep.
He cares for his people
as I care for my sheep.
He is like a loving shepherd
to his people."
So David made up his new song.
It began,
   "The Lord is my Shepherd,"
and it told how God cares for his people
just as David cared for his sheep.

★   ★   ★   ★   ★   ★

Still today, people love to sing
David's famous song.
Still today, they sing
"The Lord is my Shepherd."

The Boy who Saved a Swan

This is a legend about a wise man
who lived in India long, long ago.
The people of India called him Buddha,
which means "The Wise One",
for he spent his life
teaching people how to live
and be happy.
This story is about Buddha
when he was a boy.

*　　*　　*　　*　　*　　*

Long ago in the land of India,
there lived a king and queen.
The king and queen were very happy,
for their first child had been born.
The child was a boy
and they called him Siddartha.
The king was very pleased.
    "Now I have a son

to rule over my kingdom after me,"
he said.

Siddartha grew up
into a fine strong boy.
He liked to go riding
on his favourite horse
and he enjoyed hunting deer
with his friends.
But once, when he and his friends
had caught a frightened deer,
Siddartha let the deer go free.
He did not want it to be hurt.
He did not want it to feel pain.

When Siddartha was still a boy,
he felt pain himself
for the very first time.

He was playing in the splendid gardens
of the palace with his cousin,
a boy named Devadatta.
Suddenly a flock of wild swans
flew over the palace gardens.
The swans were on their way
to the mountains.
It was springtime
and they were going to the mountains
to make their nests.
The beautiful white birds
called to each other
as they flew across
the clear blue sky.

Quickly Devadatta picked up
his bow and arrows
and let fly with an arrow.
The arrow hit the first swan
in one of its great white wings.
The swan could not fly

with an arrow in its wing
and it began to fall.
Down, down, down it fell
until it hit the ground.
It fell among the sweet-scented roses
in the palace gardens.
There it lay, quiet and still.
Its beautiful white wing
was spotted with blood
and the cruel arrow
was still fixed in it.

Siddartha ran to the wounded bird.
It was very frightened.
It snapped at Siddartha with its beak
and flapped its other wing in fright.
But Siddartha did not mind.
He knew that the swan had snapped in fear.
He sat down on the ground
and gently lifted the swan on to his lap.
He stroked it softly with his left hand.

With his right hand
he carefully pulled out the arrow.
He poured honey on the swan's wound
to heal it
and covered the wound with leaves
to keep it cool.

For some time Siddartha sat there,
comforting the wounded bird.
He wondered how the arrow
had felt to the bird,
for Siddartha had never felt pain.
He pressed the sharp point
of the cruel arrow into his own arm.
Now he knew the pain
that the swan had felt.
There were tears in Siddartha's eyes
as he comforted the wounded swan.

★　　★　　★　　★　　★　　★

After he had shot the swan,
Devadatta went to his own home.
Later that day he sent a messenger
to Siddartha.

"O Siddartha," said the messenger.
"Prince Devadatta shot a swan
which fell here in your garden.
He wants the body of the swan
for a feast.
Will you give it to him?"

"No," said Siddartha.
"If the swan was dead
its body would belong
to Prince Devadatta who killed it.
But the swan is not dead.
It is alive.
I have cared for it and loved it
and helped it to live.
Now the swan is mine.
If my cousin does not agree with me,
let him call the wise men together.
Let them say who should have the swan."

Devadatta did not agree,
so the wise men met together.
They talked for a long time.
At last one of them said,

"Siddartha has saved the swan's life.

He has loved and cared for it.
The swan is his by right.
Devadatta has no right to the swan."
   All the wise men agreed
that the swan belonged to Siddartha.
So Siddartha kept the swan.
He loved and cared for it
until it was ready
to fly off to the mountains.

*   *   *   *   *   *

A few days later
the king sent for Siddartha.
   "My son," said the king,
"let us go riding together.
Springtime is the most beautiful time
of all the year.
Let us ride together
through this lovely country
which one day will be yours."
   So Siddartha and his father
rode out together on their fine horses.

They saw farmers ploughing the land.
They saw sowers scattering the seed.
They saw the smith
hammering at his forge.
They saw the bees busy at their work.
They watched the squirrels
as they scampered about in play.
They heard the songs of the birds
as they made their nests.
They heard drums and music
in the villages
where the people danced and made merry.
Every living creature seemed busy
and happy in the warm spring sunshine.

"How wonderful everything is!"
said the king.
"There is beauty everywhere."

Siddartha saw the beauty,
but he saw other things too.
He saw things his father did not see.
Siddartha saw the pain
of the poor ploughmen.
He saw how hard they had to work
to grow enough food to keep alive.
Siddartha saw the pain of the oxen
as they dragged the heavy ploughs.
He watched the ploughmen
drive them on with cruel whips
and he felt their pain himself.

Siddartha saw how animals
brought pain to each other.
The lizard fed on ants.
The snake fed on the lizard,
and the kite bird caught the snake.

Siddartha saw all the beauty
and the wonder that his father saw,
but he saw all the pain too.
He felt the pain in his heart.

*　　*　　*　　*　　*　　*

When they got back to the palace
Siddartha went into the beautiful gardens
and sat under a shady tree.
He wanted to think
about all he had seen.
The sky grew dark as night came
but Siddartha was still
in the garden.
He was still sitting
under the tree,

thinking about all he had seen.

Why was there so much beauty
in the world?
Why was there so much pain?
These were the questions which puzzled him
and he knew he had to find the answers.

When he grew up Siddartha wandered
from place to place.
He talked to the men and women he met,
and he thought about the world.
At last he found the answers
he was looking for.
Then he taught people how to live.
He taught them how to be happy
in a world where there was
so much pain.
People called him Buddha—
"The Wise One".
And still today
Buddhists all over the world
follow the teachings of Lord Buddha,
who once loved and cared for
a wounded swan.

Presents for the Poor

This is another legend
about the wise teacher, Buddha.

   ★ ★ ★ ★ ★ ★

One day Buddha sat under a tree
to collect presents for the poor.
People brought gifts to him
to show their love for the poor.
First came the king.

"Lord Buddha," said the king.
"My gift is the big house
you can see beyond the river
and all the land around it."

Then came the prince.

"Lord Buddha," he said.
I bring you these rich jewels
to give to the poor."

Then came the lords,
bringing gold and silver.

They were followed by merchants
who brought bags of money.
  When all these rich men
came to him with their gifts,
Buddha did not stand up
to thank them.
He took their gifts and
held out his right hand to thank them.
  After the rich men had given their gifts
an old woman came to Buddha.
She was thin and bent
and dressed in rags.
In her hand she held a small orange.
  "Lord Buddha," she said,
"I am a poor old woman

and I have nothing in the world.
All I have is this orange
which a kind man gave me.
I was just going to eat it
when I heard that you were collecting
presents for the poor.
So I did not eat the orange
and came at once
to give it to you.
Please, Lord Buddha, take it for the poor."

At once Buddha got up
and went to her.
He held out both hands to her
to receive her orange
and to say thank you to her.

The king and the prince

and the lords and the merchants
were very surprised.
They could not understand
why Buddha had thanked the old woman
more than he had thanked them.

"Lord Buddha," said the king,
"we all brought you rich gifts
but you did not stand up to thank us.
You only held out your right hand.
The old woman brought only a little gift
but you stood up and went to her
and took her little gift with both hands.
Why did you do that?"

Buddha looked at the king and the prince
and at the rich lords and merchants.
Then he said to them,
"You are all rich men.
You gave only a little of what you have.
The old woman is poor,
but she gave everything she had.
Her love is far greater than yours
so I thanked her more
than I thanked you."

A Journey to Remember

The next four stories are about Jesus,
a great teacher who lived
about two thousand years ago.
The first story is about a time
when Jesus was twelve years old.
It is a story from real life.

*   *   *   *   *   *

There was once a boy
whose name was Jesus.
He lived in the small town of Nazareth.
   One day Jesus woke up early.
He was excited, for it was a very special day.
Jesus was twelve years old
and he was going on a long journey
with his family
for the very first time.
They were going to Jerusalem,
a big city far away.

In Jerusalem was the Temple,
and Jesus and his family
were going there to pray to God.
They were going to a festival
which took place at a special time each
spring.   This festival was called Passover.
Jesus had never been to Jerusalem before
and now he was going there
for the Passover Festival.
No wonder he was excited!

Many families were travelling
from Nazareth to Jerusalem
and everybody was up early
to get ready for the journey.
Outside every house in Nazareth
the family donkey was waiting patiently.

The donkeys carried everything
the families needed for the journey:
a tent to sleep in,
mattresses for sleeping on,
pots for cooking,
drinking water and food.

At last everyone was ready.
The donkeys were loaded and they all set off.
As the people walked along the road
they kept close together.
They were afraid of the robbers
who hid in the hills
waiting for lonely travellers.

When the sun climbed high in the sky
it was too hot for walking and
everyone stopped to rest.
Jesus ate his meal with his family.
Then he went off to be with his friends.
His mother, Mary, did not worry about him.
She knew Jesus would be quite safe
because all the other families
were friends from Nazareth.

In the afternoon they went on again.

Soon the sun began to drop behind the hills
and the travellers found a place
to stop for the night.
Everyone helped to put up the tents
and to light the fires.
The donkeys were tired.
They needed rest and food and water.

Soon the smell of cooking
brought families together for supper.
It was the best meal of the day
and Mary had made a fine stew.
After supper Jesus snuggled down
on his mattress, but he was far too excited
to sleep much that night.

Everyone was up early next morning.
They ate a quick breakfast of bread and figs
so that they could be on the road
before the sun grew hot.
Jesus spent most of the day
with his friends,
but Mary did not worry.
She knew that he would be quite safe.

Mary did not see Jesus again

until he came back in the evening
to eat his supper.
That night was even more exciting.
Jesus knew that the next day
he would see Jerusalem.

Morning came at last
and everyone hurried to set off again.
They all wanted to see Jerusalem
and this was the most exciting part
of the journey.
The road went downhill.
It twisted and turned like a snake
and the boys raced ahead.
Bend followed bend,
but still they raced on.
Each of them wanted to be the first
to see the Holy City of Jerusalem.

Then, at last, they saw it.
Jerusalem stood before them,
high on its hill,
with strong walls around it.
The white houses shone
in the bright sunshine

and above the houses they could see
the beautiful Temple.
The sun shone on its stones of white marble
and on its roof of glittering gold.
Jesus and his friends
were filled with wonder.
They had not dreamed
that anything could be so beautiful.
The city was crowded with people
from many lands

and the families from Nazareth
put up their tents outside the city.
They stayed there for a week
and each day they went into the city
to visit the Temple.

At the Temple were wise men,
and Jesus and the other boys
talked with them each day.
They talked about their school in Nazareth.
They talked about the books
they had been reading.
The wise men were interested
to hear what the boys had to say
and to answer their questions.

At last the week was over.
All the families from Nazareth
loaded their donkeys
and got ready for the long journey home.
Early in the morning they set off for
Nazareth.   The children walked together.
They had much to talk about.
Mary did not worry
that Jesus was not with her.

She knew he would be safe
with his friends.

Evening came and it was time for supper.
Still there was no sign of Jesus.
He did not come to the tent
and Mary began to wonder where he was.
She went to all the other tents,
looking for her son.

"No, he's not with us," everyone said.
"We haven't seen him today."
Mary got more and more worried
as she hurried from tent to tent.
Jesus was not in any of them.
He was not to be found.

The next morning Mary got up very early
and hurried back to Jerusalem.
She asked everyone she knew
if they had seen her son, Jesus.
Nobody had seen Jesus
and for three days Mary searched for him.
She grew more and more worried.

Then she thought of the wise men.
She remembered that Jesus had spent all his
time in the Temple with them.
They might know where he was.
She hurried back to the part of the Temple
where Jesus had sat with the wise men.
The wise men were there,
and Jesus was with them.
He was listening to the wise men
and asking them questions.

"Jesus!" cried Mary
as she hurried towards him.
"I have searched everywhere for you.
I have been so worried about you."
Jesus was surprised
when he heard his mother's words.

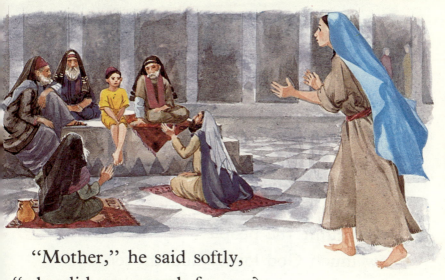

"Mother," he said softly,
"why did you search for me?
Didn't you know
that I would be here in the Temple?"

Mary was puzzled, but she said nothing.
She had been angry and upset
but now her worries turned to joy.

So Jesus left the wise men in the Temple
and went back to Nazareth with his family.
The Passover Festival was over
for another year, but Jesus
had much to remember.
He would never forget his first visit
to the beautiful city of Jerusalem.

Jesus Makes New Friends

When Jesus grew up
he became a great teacher.
People came from far and near
to listen to his teaching.
Jesus loved children,
and in this story
he is telling the people
how much God loves children, too.

*   *   *   *   *   *

David and his sister Ruth
lived in a small town
in the land we now call Israel.
Their house was near the market-place,
where people went
to buy all kinds of things.
In the market-place
there was a big, open space.
It was a fine place for people
to meet and sit and talk,

and for children to run and play.

David and Ruth often went to the
market-place after school to play with their
friends. Their best friends were Peter and
Sarah, who lived next door to them.

One day David and Peter
dashed out of school.
They ran to the market-place to play.
As they came near
David saw a man sitting there,
with his friends around him.
David had not seen this man
in the market-place before
and he stood and stared.
The man looked at David and then
smiled at him.

"What is your name?" he asked.

"I'm David."

"Come and sit with me, David,"
the man said.
He had such a kind face
that David was not afraid.

The man sat David on his knee
and put his arms around him.
Then the kind man began
to talk to his friends,
and to the people from the town.
He spoke to them about God's love for
them.   Then he turned to David
and the other children
who were listening to him.
He told them how God cared for
all children and loved them.

When David got home
he told his mother about the kind man
in the market-place.

"I know who that man is,"
said David's mother.
"His name is Jesus,
and he is a good man, a man of God."

David never forgot the man
with the kind face
and one day, when he was bigger,
he saw Jesus again.
It happened in the market-place.
The children had gone there
to play as usual.
David and Ruth went there
with Peter and Sarah.
They found other friends
in the market-place,
and soon they were playing
their favourite games together.

Then all at once it became very quiet.
The children stopped their playing.
They looked round

to see what had happened.
Suddenly David saw
the man with the kind face.

David ran back to his house quickly.

"Mother! Mother!" he cried,
"Jesus has come!
He's in the market-place
talking to the people."
David's mother had longed to meet Jesus.
She quickly called her neighbour,
the mother of Peter and Sarah.
The two mothers hurried
to the market-place and called
their children to them.
They joined the crowd around Jesus.

By now it was a big crowd,
and they were right at the back.
The two mothers tried
to get through the crowd.
They wanted to take their children
near to Jesus.
But Jesus's friends stopped them.

"Don't bother Jesus now," they said.

"You can see how busy he is.
He has come a long way
and he is very tired."
The two mothers turned away sadly.
Then suddenly they heard
the voice of Jesus.
He was cross with his friends.
"Let the children come to me!"
he said angrily.
"Do not turn them away!"
Then the people made way for
the two mothers to come through the crowd.
They came to Jesus with their children.
Jesus took each child in his arms,
one after the other.
He took Ruth and Sarah,
and David and Peter,
and he blessed each one of them.
The children were too young
to understand who Jesus was.
But they knew
he was a friend of children.

Jesus Helps a Little Girl

Jesus was not just a good teacher.
He was always helping people, too.
This story tells how he helped
to make a little girl well again.

*   *   *   *   *   *

Peter, James and John were fishermen.
They lived in Israel
and fished in the Sea of Galilee.
Jesus often went with them in their boat,
for they were his friends.
　　One day, Jesus and his friends
were coming back in the boat
to the town where they lived.
A lot of people were waiting for them
on the shore.
They had come to see Jesus,
for they loved to listen to his stories.
　　When the boat reached the shore,

Jesus stood up and began
to talk to the people.
He talked to them about God,
and the people listened quietly.

Suddenly there was a noise
at the back of the crowd.
Someone was trying to make his way
through the crowd to the boat
where Jesus was talking.
It was a man called Jairus.

Jairus was very troubled
and he wanted to speak to Jesus.
When Jairus got to the boat
he fell on his knees in front of Jesus.
Tears were pouring down his face.

"Master," he sobbed,
"it's my little daughter Susanna.
She is only twelve years old
and she is very ill.
I think she is dying.
If only you will
come and see her,
I know that she will live."

Jesus felt very sorry for Jairus
and said in a kind voice,
"I will come at once."

Then Jesus and his three friends
left the crowd of people
and went with Jairus.
They followed him to
the narrow street
where he lived.
When they were nearly there,

they saw a man hurrying towards them.
It was the servant of Jairus.

"Susanna is dead, Sir,"
he said to Jairus.

"Why bother the Master any more?
There is nothing he can do
for her now."
Jesus heard what the servant said,
and he said to Jairus,

"Do not be afraid, Jairus.
Trust me.   Your daughter will be
all right."
Then Jesus followed Jairus into the house.

It was filled with people.
All his family and many
of his friends were there.
They all wanted to be with Jairus
and his wife at this sad time.
Some were playing sad music
on their flutes,
others were weeping and wailing,
and crying out loud.

When they saw Jesus

they became quiet for a moment.
Jesus asked them,
   "Why are you making all this noise?
The little girl is not dead.
She is sleeping."
The people in the house laughed at Jesus,
for they had seen Susanna
lying pale and still
and they were sure that she was dead.
Jesus turned to Jairus and said sternly,
   "Send all these people
out of your house."
The people went away
and the house became quiet.

Then Jesus went in to see Susanna
with her mother and father.
His three friends, Peter, James and John,
were there too.
Jesus knelt by the bed
where Susanna lay.
She was pale and still
and it seemed that she was dead.
Jesus took Susanna's hand in his.

"Little girl," he said gently,
"it is time for you to wake up."
Susanna gave a deep sigh.
She stirred and slowly opened her eyes
and then she smiled.

In a moment she was sitting up
and she was quite well again.

Jairus and his wife could not
believe their eyes.
How happy they were!
Jesus said to them,

"Give Susanna something to eat,
and do not tell anyone
what has happened here today."

Then Jesus called Peter, James and John
and they went back to the shore.
The crowd was still there, waiting for Jesus.
He was very tired,
but he did not want
to disappoint the people.
So, again he talked about God.
He told the people the stories
they always loved to hear.
He did not rest until they had all gone away.

The Girl who Lost a Treasure

Many of the stories that Jesus told
were about God.
By talking about everyday things
which people knew well,
Jesus helped them to understand
important things about God.
Stories like these are called parables.
This parable was made up by Jesus
to help us understand
something about God.

* * * * * *

Rachel was very happy.
She had been married only a few weeks
and now she had her own little house
where she lived with her husband.
 Rachel was very proud of her new home.
She kept it clean and tidy.
Often, as she was doing her work,

she liked to think about her wedding day.
What a lovely day it had been!
She remembered
her beautiful wedding dress.
She remembered how all her family
and friends had come to her wedding,
and how happy they all were.

She remembered all the fine presents
she had been given.
The finest present of all
was a chain made of ten silver coins.
Her mother and father had given it to
Rachel on her wedding day.
Rachel treasured the chain
more than anything else
because it showed that she was married.

Rachel wore the chain of coins
over the veil on her head.
The veil was a pretty cloth
which covered her head and neck.
It protected her from the burning sun.
The chain of coins kept her veil in place.
How proud she was to wear it!

One morning Rachel washed her face
and brushed her hair as usual.
Next she put her pretty veil
over her head as she always did.
Then she took her chain of coins
to put over her veil.
As she picked up the chain
she saw that one of the coins was missing.
Rachel was horrified.
She had lost one of her silver coins!

"I must find it!"
she said to herself.
"I'll search and search and search.

I'll search everywhere.
I can't do anything else
until I've found my precious coin."
   Rachel waited until her husband
had finished his breakfast.
When he had gone to work on the farm
she began her search.
Rachel knew she must have lost the coin
somewhere in the house.
   "It must be on the floor,"
she thought to herself.
   The house was one big room.
It had only earth for a floor
so there was a lot of dust.
Rachel would have to sweep
all over this dusty floor
to look for her lost treasure.
   The house was dark.
It had only one small window,
and that was high up in the wall,
so that the burning sun could not get in.
Before Rachel began to sweep
she filled the lamp with oil

and lit the wick.
Its light shone brightly
across the dark room.

Rachel's broom was made of big leaves
from a palm tree.
They were tied to a stick
which she used for a handle.
She swept slowly and carefully
all over the ground.
It took Rachel a long time
to sweep right through the house.
She swept and searched
until her arms ached
and her eyes were tired.
Still she could not find her precious coin.

"I'll start again,"
said Rachel to herself.
"I must not give up.
I must go on searching
until I find it."
So Rachel began her
search all over again.

This time she took the
lamp and went down on her knees.
She put the lamp beside her
and used her hands to sift through the dust.
Slowly she moved over the ground,
sifting and searching.
She searched until her knees hurt
and her fingers were sore.
Then, suddenly,
she saw something shining
in the thick dust by the wall.
At last Rachel had found
her lost treasure!
How happy and excited she was!
She rushed to the door,
and called out to her neighbours.

"Mary! Rebecca! Come quickly!
I lost one of my silver coins
and now I've found it again!
Come and share my joy!"
Rachel's neighbours all came hurrying
to her house.
What a party they had!
How happy they all were!
They shared Rachel's joy
for they would have felt like Rachel
if one of them had lost a silver coin.

How happy Rachel was
to have found her coin.
She was more happy
over the coin she had lost and found,
than over all the other coins
still safe on her chain.

★　　★　　★　　★　　★　　★

Jesus told this parable long ago.
It was really a story about God.
　"God is your Father,"
Jesus was saying to the people.
"You are his children.
He loves you
just as a father loves his own children.
How sad God is
when his children forget him.
But how happy he is
when they come back to him
and want to be friends again.
It is like losing a treasure
and finding it again."

Surprises

This story is a legend
about a good man
who loved helping poor and sick people.
He lived a long time after Jesus,
but he believed in Jesus
and followed his teaching.

★   ★   ★   ★   ★   ★

Many years ago,
in a far-off land,
there lived a good man
whose name was Nicholas.
  Nicholas was a bishop
in charge of a church.
His work was to care for
the people of his church
and to show them the love of God
by the way he lived.
He was good and kind
and the people loved him.

One day Nicholas heard
about a poor cobbler
who lived in his town.
The cobbler made boots and shoes
and, when they had holes in them,
he mended them.
He worked hard to get enough money
to feed his family.

The cobbler had a wife and
three daughters.
His three daughters were growing up
and it was time for them to marry.
They wanted to marry and have
homes and children of their own.
But they could not find
husbands who would marry them
because they were too poor.

In those days, when a girl married
she had to bring money to her husband.
The poor cobbler had no money to spare.
So his three daughters
had no money to bring to husbands.
This made them sad,

for they would never be able to
get married. They would never have
husbands and homes and
children of their own.

When Nicholas heard this story
he was sorry for the cobbler's daughters.
He made secret plans to help them.
He collected money until he had
three bags full of gold.
One night he went secretly
to the cobbler's house.
He dropped the bags
through the open window.
They fell on the floor
where the three girls
left their shoes at night.

When they got up in the morning
each girl found a bag of gold
by her shoes.
Now they could all marry
and have husbands and homes
and children of their own.

*   *   *   *   *   *

Nicholas was always helping people.
He wanted to keep his good deeds secret
but, somehow, people always found out.
They all knew about his kindness
and they all loved him.
    Stories of his love and kindness
spread far and wide.

When Nicholas died
he was made a Saint.
This meant that
people would remember
his goodness and love for ever.

One special day in the year was kept
to remember Saint Nicholas.
It was the 6th of December
and it was called
the Festival of Saint Nicholas.
On that day people went to church
to thank God for Saint Nicholas.

After they had been to church,
they feasted and danced
at home and in the streets.
Best of all, they gave presents.
They gave them secretly at night
just as Saint Nicholas gave presents
secretly and at night.
It became a custom
to give presents,
especially to children,
on the Festival of Saint Nicholas.

The Festival of Saint Nicholas
was kept in many lands.
Children in the Netherlands
looked forward eagerly
to the coming of Saint Nicholas.
They believed that he came
dressed in the red cloak of a bishop.
His servant, Black Peter, came with him,
dressed all in black.
The children thought that
Saint Nicholas and Black Peter
travelled through the night,
over the roof tops.
They dropped presents down the chimneys
so that they would fall into the shoes
which the children had left
beside the fireplace.
Still today, in the Netherlands,
the Festival of Saint Nicholas
is a wonderful time for children.
Each year someone dressed as Saint Nicholas
arrives in a boat.
With him is someone else

dressed as his servant, Black Peter.
They sail into the harbour of Amsterdam,
the beautiful capital of the Netherlands.
Then Saint Nicholas rides on a white horse
to the royal palace
in the centre of Amsterdam.
The Queen of the Netherlands
welcomes him to the palace.

*   *   *   *   *   *

On the sixth day of December
all the children in the Netherlands
wait eagerly for their presents.
The presents are called "surprises".

They are carefully wrapped up
and made into parcels.
The children cannot tell
what is inside the wrapping paper.
Sometimes the presents
are hidden in strange places.
But each surprise has a little greeting
from Saint Nicholas.

*   *   *   *   *   *

The people of the Netherlands
do not say "Saint Nicholas".
In their way of speaking
his name is "Sinter Klaas".
Sometimes we use the name "Santa Claus"
for Father Christmas,
who secretly brings presents to children
on Christmas Eve.
   Our story of Santa Claus
comes from the story of Sinter Klaas,
or the good Saint Nicholas,
who gave presents secretly by night
to the three daughters of the poor cobbler.

New Life at Easter

Have you ever wondered
why we have Easter eggs?
Easter is a Christian festival.
It comes in the springtime,
when new life is bursting out
all around us.
Suddenly the trees are covered
with tiny, green buds.
Brightly-coloured flowers
open out in the warm sunshine.

Young lambs frisk and play
in the fields, and baby birds hatch out
from their eggs.

The Easter festival
is about new life too.
Christians believe that,
on the very first Easter Sunday,
Jesus came alive again
after he had died on the Cross.
So Easter eggs remind Christians
of the time when Jesus
came alive again.

Secrets

Long ago, in the land of Germany,
there was a village
where everybody was very poor.
The families who lived there
had always been poor.
The mothers never had much money,
but each year they always managed
to buy presents for their children
on Easter Sunday.
   Then a year came
when they had no money at all.
All the mothers were worried
because it would soon be Easter
and they could not buy sweets
for their children.
Each day the mothers talked together.
Each day they tried to think of something.
One mother said,
   "Whatever can we do about
presents for our children
on Easter Sunday?

We have no money to buy sweets
for them, this year."

Another mother said,

"I have an idea.
What about giving them eggs?
The hens are laying well
and we have plenty of eggs."

"Oh no," said another mother,
"we cannot give them
ordinary eggs for presents."

The mothers fell silent.
They thought and thought
about what to do,
but they could not think
of what to give the children
for their Easter presents.

Then one day, just before Easter Sunday,
one of the mothers said,

"I've got an idea."
The mothers gathered around her
and listened to her idea.
They nodded to each other.
They smiled to each other.

They whispered to each other.
Then they hurried off
to tell their secret
to all the mothers of the village.
They made sure
that no children heard them.
They wanted to keep their secret,
so that the children would have a surprise
on Easter Sunday.

★　　★　　★　　★　　★　　★

On Easter Sunday it was bright and sunny.
The mothers of the village
got up early in the morning.
They came out of their houses
and hurried to the woods.
Each mother carried a basket
with a brightly-coloured cloth over it.
　　When they came back from the woods
the bright cloths were tied
over their heads.　They looked
just like the head scarves
they often wore.

Their baskets were filled
with wild flowers from the woods,
so everyone could see
why the mothers had been there.
They had been to get flowers for Easter.
No one knew there was another reason
why they had been to the woods that
morning.   The mothers smiled to each other
as they thought about their secret.

　　After breakfast all the villagers
walked to their church
for the Easter Sunday service.
The children chattered to each other
as they went.

"My mother went to the woods
early this morning," said one.

"My mother went too," said another.

"And mine," said another.
Soon they found
that all their mothers
had been to the woods
to fill their baskets with Easter flowers.
But there was nothing strange about that.
Mothers always decorated their homes
for Easter Day,
and they always used spring flowers.

Soon the service was over.
The children skipped happily
out of church.
They had been quiet and still
while they were in church.
Now they wanted to run and jump
and play with their friends.
Besides, they were looking forward
to their Easter presents.
The mothers said to their children,

"Off you go now!

We are going to be busy
getting dinner ready.
You can go and play in the woods.
You might find some surprises."

The children hurried off to the woods
where their mothers had been
early in the morning.
They played games.
They climbed trees.
They explored good hiding-places.
The woods were filled
with happy shouts and laughter.
Suddenly one of the children called out,
"Here! Come and see
what I've found."
The children ran to see what it was.
It was a red egg!
No one had ever seen a red egg before.
They all stared at it in wonder.
"Let's see if we can find some more,"
said one of them.
Soon they were all hunting busily.
They hunted in the long grass,

they hunted under the bushes,
they hunted round the trees.
They found many more coloured eggs.
They found red ones and blue ones,
yellow ones and brown ones.
They found eggs
of all the colours of the rainbow.

Soon everyone had found some.
Their pockets were full
of the gaily-coloured eggs.
They even carried them in their hats!

Now they were in a hurry
to get home for their dinner.
They couldn't wait
to show their fathers and mothers
the treasures they had found.

As they were hurrying back
through the woods,
one of the boys said,

"I wonder what kind of eggs
they can be?"

"They are not from wild birds,"
said one girl,
who knew all about wild birds.
"They are too big for that."

"They are the same size as hen's eggs,"
said another boy.

"But hens don't lay coloured eggs,"
said another.

Suddenly a hare dashed out
in front of the children.
They had scared it
and the hare was running for safety.

"That's it!" cried one of the children.
"They must be hares' eggs!
Hares must lay coloured eggs!"
All the children laughed.
Of course they knew

that hares do not lay eggs,
but they liked the joke.

"Hares' eggs!   Hares' eggs!"
they began to shout.
"We've got hares' eggs."

As they came back to the village
they were still laughing
and singing together.

"Hares' eggs for Easter!
Hares' eggs for Easter!
We've got hares' eggs!"
The mothers smiled
as they watched their happy children
come skipping home
from the woods for dinner.
How pleased the mothers were.
It had taken them a long time
to boil the eggs until they were hard
and then to paint them in gay colours.
Now they knew it had all been worth while.
They had kept their Easter secret
and the children had
their Easter presents after all.

Easter Games

Children in many lands
play games with their Easter eggs.
One game is called "Egg-tapping".
Each child holds an Easter egg
in his hand.
Then one child taps
the pointed end of his friend's egg
with his own egg.
A·sharp tap
can make the other egg crack.
But he must be careful.
He may crack his own egg instead!
The child whose egg cracks first
is the loser.

★　　★　　★　　★　　★　　★

Another game with Easter eggs
is called "Egg-rolling".
The eggs for this game
are boiled to make them hard.

They are all painted in bright colours
and some have patterns on them.
All the eggs look different
and the children all know
their own eggs.

First the players find a hill
where the grass is not too long.
Then they roll their coloured eggs
down the hill.
The winner is the child whose egg
is the first to reach
the bottom of the hill.

Festival Cards

Inside the school hall
it was warm and dry.
Outside, the wind blew
and the rain splashed.
It was a cold, wet day in December,
but it was a very special day
for Sharon and Mark.
They had both been looking
forward to it for a long time.
It was their birthday.
Sharon and Mark had been born
on the same day.
Now they were looking forward
to the end of School Assembly.
    At last the Headteacher said,
    "And now it's time for birthdays.
Who has a birthday today?"
This was the moment
Sharon and Mark had been waiting for.
Up went their hands.

"Come and show us your cards,"
said the Headteacher.
Sharon and Mark went to the front.
They gave their birthday cards
to the Headteacher.
How proud they felt!
Some cards had a big 8 on them,
because Sharon and Mark
were 8 years old today.

The Headteacher showed the cards
to the rest of the children.
Then she spoke to the children.

"Do you remember the word we use
for a special day like a birthday?"
Some children remembered the word
and said it together—"Festival".

"Yes, a festival is a day
when we remember something special.
Some festivals are shared by people
all over the world.
Which festival is like that?"

"Christmas!" cried everyone,
for it was December and the school

was already making plans for Christmas.

"That's right," said the Headteacher.
"Christmas is the birthday of Jesus.
It is a festival for Christians.
Christians all over the world
share this happy time.
When Christmas comes
they say 'Happy Christmas'
to each other.

"Today is the birthday of Sharon and
Mark. It is their own special festival.
So let's all wish them
a very happy day."
And all the children joined in with,

"Happy Birthday, Sharon.
Happy Birthday, Mark."

★　　★　　★　　★　　★　　★

Christmas soon came.
All week the children were busy
making decorations
for their Christmas party.

They made Christmas cards too.
First they chose a picture
for the front of the card.
There were pictures of Baby Jesus
in the stable at Bethlehem.
Some showed Mary, his mother.
Others showed the shepherds.
Some showed the wise men,
with their presents for the baby.

There were pictures of winter, too.
Some showed trees covered with snow.
Some showed robins looking for food.
Some showed holly with bright red berries.

Then there were pictures of happy people.
Some showed children opening presents.
Some showed people
enjoying their Christmas dinner.
Some showed people singing carols
round the Christmas tree.
There were all kinds of pictures
and every picture was different.

Then the children wrote
"Happy Christmas" and other

Christmas greetings on their cards.
They made cards
for their mothers and fathers,
and for their grandparents,
and for their uncles and aunts.
They made Christmas cards
for their special friends, too.

The children liked to give cards
which they had made themselves.
Cards they had made themselves were
special.   Their family and friends

enjoyed them much more
than cards from shops.
They knew the children had made them
with great care and love.

   ★ ★ ★ ★ ★ ★

While the children
were making their cards,
their teacher was there to help them.
 "Do people of other religions
give cards to each other
like Christians do?" asked Sharon.
 "Oh yes," said the teacher.
"They have their own festivals,
when they give cards
just as Christians do.
By giving cards they show their love
for their family and friends.
The cards carry good wishes
for the festival,
and for the future.
When do you think

would be a good time to send
good wishes for the future?"
The children thought hard.

"New Year would be a good time,"
said one of them.
The teacher said,

"That's right.   People in every land
have a New Year festival.
In Japan the New Year festival
is the biggest holiday
of the whole year.
It is called 'Ganjitsu'.
People give each other greetings cards.
They send good wishes
for the year that is just beginning."

"Does the New Year come at the same
time for everyone?" asked Mark.

"Oh no," said their teacher.
"Our New Year begins in January,
and it is the same in Japan.
But for many people
the New Year festival comes
at a different time.

New Year for the Jews
comes in September or October.
Jews live in many lands,
but wherever they live,
they have their own New Year festival.
They call it 'Rosh Hashanah'.

"In India, people of the Hindu religion
have their New Year festival
in October or November.
They call it 'Diwali'.
At their New Year festival
they light lamps.
Each house has bright lights

to welcome their great Goddess, Lakshmi.
People of the Sikh religion
keep the festival of Diwali too.

"So New Year festivals come
at different times.
But at all these festivals
people give cards to their family
and their friends.   In this way
they show their love and send good wishes
for the festival and the future.
So you see, people everywhere
give cards of greeting.
It is a lovely way
to remember a festival, isn't it?"

The children thought so too.
They carried on making their Christmas
cards.   Now they worked even harder.
They wanted their cards to be the finest
they had ever made.
They wanted to show their family and
friends that they really meant it
when they wished them
"Happy Christmas!"

Stories in this Book

Everyone loves a story.
When you were young
you loved fairy stories.
Now you are older
you like other stories.
There are many different
kinds of stories,
and you have found some of them
as you have been reading this book.
There are no fairy stories
in this book,
but there are stories of other kinds.
What kinds of stories are they?

Stories of Real-life

One kind of story
is about people who really lived,
and about things that really happened.
They are "real-life" stories—
like the story of the

shepherd boy who became King David.
Real-life stories are not made up.
They really happened.
They are stories of real people
who became great and famous.

Stories called Legends
Other stories grew up
about famous people, too,
but these were not real-life stories.
They were legends.
These stories showed
how great their heroes were
and told of wonders
and adventures
and brave deeds.

Legends may be about people
who really lived,
but we cannot be sure
that they tell of things
that really happened.

One story in this book
tells how a baby named Moses

was saved from being killed.
We cannot be sure
that this really happened.
But Moses was a real person
and when he grew up he became
the great leader of his people.

Stories called Parables
Some stories are made up.
They are not stories about
people who really lived.

They are not stories about
things that really happened.
But that does not matter a bit,
for these stories were made up
to help us understand something else.
Stories like these are called parables.

The parable in this book
tells of a girl
who lost a wedding present,
and of how she looked everywhere for it.
This story was made up by Jesus
to help us understand something
about God.

Stories of Beginnings

When we are young
we ask lots of questions.
The world seems very big to us
and full of things
we want to know about.
So we ask questions
to find out more about them.

We ask questions about
how things began,
and where things came from.
And these questions
are hard to answer.

Stories grew up about beginnings.
These are not real-life stories.
They are stories
of what people believed
long ago.

"What's that?" asks a child,
seeing a rainbow for the first time.
A story in this book
tells what people
in lands of the North
believed about the rainbow.

Another hard question is—
"How did the world begin?
Where did it come from?"
Another story in this book
tells what Indians of North America
believed about how the world began.

Stories about Special Times

The most important day in the year for you
is your birthday.
It is your own special time.
But there are other special times
in each year
which we can share together.
We call these special times "Festivals".

Your birthday is your very own festival,
but all over the world,
people have festivals
which they share together.
There is a story in this book
about the festival of Christmas.

It tells how Christmas presents began,
and how the people of the Netherlands
share their special time together.

Different Kinds of Stories
As you have been reading this book
you have found
five different kinds of stories—
> Stories of Real-life,
> Stories called Legends,
> Stories called Parables,
> Stories of Beginnings,
> Stories about Special Times.

Each kind of story is important,
for they each tell us something different.